Erastus Brigham Bigelow

The Tariff Policy of England and of the United States

Contrasted

Erastus Brigham Bigelow

The Tariff Policy of England and of the United States Contrasted

ISBN/EAN: 9783337187873

Printed in Europe, USA, Canada, Australia, Japan

Cover: Foto ©Suzi / pixelio.de

More available books at **www.hansebooks.com**

THE

TARIFF POLICY

OF

ENGLAND AND OF THE UNITED STATES CONTRASTED.

BY

ERASTUS B. BIGELOW.

BOSTON:

LITTLE, BROWN, AND COMPANY.

1877.

(

NOTE.

SOME of the tables of statistics, and some of the arguments in this pamphlet, are taken from the author's work entitled, "The Tariff Question Considered in Regard to the Policy of England and the Interests of the United States," published in 1862.

Other statistical statements and numerical comparisons, giving results of more recent date, were compiled expressly for the pamphlet. In all cases, the statistical facts are derived from official sources.

E. B. B.

Boston, September, 1877.

CONTENTS.

THE TARIFF POLICY

OF

ENGLAND AND THE UNITED STATES.

THERE is a prevailing expectation that our customs tariff will be revised by the next Congress. As such legislation will have a direct bearing on the prosperity of the country, it is important that the probable effects of proposed changes should be clearly understood. Theoretical and partisan discussion of the subject will do but little towards that end. Nor will the experience of other nations be a safe guide for us. The conditions of production are so various in different countries that the customs tariff of every nation should be determined by its own interests and needs.

There is no ultimate principle of universal application, involved either in free trade or protection. They are questions of policy. Free trade in England, and protection in the United States, have been so much discussed on theoretical grounds, in disregard of facts and the peculiar condition and requirements of the respective countries, that a popular misapprehension prevails in regard to their real character. and effect.

It is my purpose to discuss these questions, in their practical relations to national interests. The free-trade maxims and example of England are so often and so zealously commended to our adoption and imitation, not only by Englishmen, but by many among ourselves, that it is especially important at this time, that we should rightly understand her tariff policy, the exigencies which from time to time determined its character, and the interest she has in urging other nations to follow her lead. These topics I will endeavor to present as they appear in the light of unquestionable facts.

THE TARIFF POLICY OF ENGLAND.

Great Britain derives her national strength mainly from her commerce; and her manufactures almost entirely sustain that commerce. This she well understands, and to protect, encourage, and extend her manufactures has been the wise and uniform policy of her statesmen for more than a century; and the result is seen in a manufacturing prosperity that is without a parallel. Although national advancement may be the constant object of a nation, the methods of its accomplishment must necessarily conform to the ever-changing conditions incident to general progress. The changes which England's tariff-policy has undergone, from time to time, exemplify this great truth. What those changes have been, and their relation to the exigencies which determined them, I will now briefly consider. They will be best understood by dividing the time of their occurrence into three epochs.

The first epoch covers the period in which manufacturing was mainly carried on by handicraft methods. During this period, the English possessed no superiority as a manufacturing people. Lower wages, cheaper living, and greater aptitude for handicraft in the inhabitants of several other countries, enabled their manufacturers to undersell the manufacturers of England. To sustain the latter under this unequal competition, bounties were offered, high duties were imposed; and, in some instances, prohibition was enforced under severe penalties.

"By the 8th of Elizabeth, ch. 3, the exporter of sheep or rams was, for the first offence, to forfeit all his goods for ever, to suffer a year's imprisonment, and then have his left hand cut off, in a market-town, upon a market-day, to be there nailed up; and, for the second offence, to be adjudged a felon, and to suffer death accordingly."

" By the 13th and 14th of Charles II., ch. 18, the exportation of wool was made felony, and the exporter subjected to the same penalties and forfeitures as a felon." [1]

In 1700, an act was passed, prohibiting the importation of India calicoes, chintzes, and muslins under a penalty, upon the seller and buyer, of £200. In 1720, it was enacted that no person could wear a printed calico without the payment of £5 for the privilege, while the seller of the article was mulcted to the extent of £20. Sixteen years later, the Act of 1720 was so far modified as to legalize the use of *mixed* prints, while the prohibition against using calicoes made wholly of cotton remained in full force. This state of things lasted nearly forty years longer. In 1774, a little more than a century ago, Parliament passed an act sanctioning the manufacture of cotton, and making it lawful to use or wear any new fabric made wholly of that material.

The second epoch embraces the period so remarkable for the invention and adoption of labor-saving machinery, and the inauguration and development of the " factory system " in Great Britain. It covers nearly all the great mechanical improvements which began with the inventions of Watt, Arkwright, Hargraves, Crompton, and Cartwright. The steam-engine, the spinning-jenny, the spinning-frame, the carding-machine, and the power-loom ushered in a new era in manufacture, and laid the foundation of those great industries which constitute the basis of England's prosperity, and control as well as characterize her social and political organizations. Perceiving early the great value and importance of these inventions and improvements, England sought to confine their use to her own people, and to that end enacted laws prohibiting, under heavy penalties, the exportation of machinery, and the emigration of skilled artisans. On machinery for the manufacture of flax, the export prohibition remained in force as late as 1842.

---

[1] Smith's " Wealth of Nations," vol. ii. p. 121.

I come now to the *third epoch*, which begins with the tariff-reform movement in England, and comes down to the present time. It is memorable as the period in which England reversed her tariff-policy. Up to the beginning of this epoch, it is certain that, in order to establish and develop her manufactures, she refused no form of aid and protection which it was in the power of government to grant. When foreign productions encroached on the home market, they were excluded by actual prohibition, or by exorbitant duties of equivalent effect. Whenever an article of English manufacture (subject, however, to internal taxes) was struggling to get a foothold in a foreign market, drawbacks were allowed; while, in cases of special need, an export bounty was paid. To prevent rival nations from sharing in the great advantages which she derived from improved processes and labor-saving machinery, she guarded with jealous care every invention and discovery.

Under this rigid and discriminating system of protection, England so increased her productive power, as, at length, to surpass all other countries, both in the quantity and in the cheapness of her manufactures, excepting those of silk. This object accomplished, it is very evident that her interests and her relations were materially changed. But why, just at this crisis in her career, did the nation, which had so long been a conspicuous adherent of the protective policy, become all at once the advocate of free trade? The answer to this interrogatory is to be found, not in any feeling of confidence England's statesmen had in the free-trade theory, — as I shall show in another part of this discussion, — but in the exigencies of her situation.

Her population had attained a density far beyond the capacity of her soil to sustain. Mr. Villiers, urging, in 1844, the repeal of the corn laws, said : " For twenty years past, we have been constantly and largely dependent on other countries for our supplies of corn."[1] Pressing the

---

[1] *Corn*, in England, comprehends all the cereal grains ; but means especially wheat, rye, oats, and barley.

same topic a year later, he declared: " The time is come when every individual soul born in Great Britain, must look to manufactures, or at least to something else than agriculture, for the means of living." [1]   Said Mr. Cobden, in debate on the corn laws: " The unskilled laboring classes are in a condition which is permanently disagreeable to the government.   Look at Ireland, where five millions of people never touch wheaten bread, — where three-fourths of the people live on roots.   In the Scotch Highlands, and in the midland counties of England, there are similar evidences of want." [2]

Concurrent with this growing dependence of England on other countries for bread, the growth of manufactures elsewhere was endangering the expansion of her commerce. Rival nations had adopted the machinery and the factory system which she had vainly attempted to monopolize, and were not only largely supplying their own people with manufactures, but were nearly abreast with her in foreign markets.   To maintain her superiority as a manufacturing nation, and thereby extend her commerce, some great change, which should reduce the cost of her manufactures, and enlarge the area for their distribution, was an evident and imperious necessity.

Absolute protection had done its work.   The duties on her principal manufactures — excepting those of silk — had become virtually inoperative, as shown by the fact that, at that time, her command of the home market was such that, for several years after they were admitted free of duty, her imports of manufactures — other than those of silk — did not materially increase. [3]   The only course open to her, so far

---

[1] Hansard, vol. lxxxi., 3d series, p. 1363.   [2] Ibid. 353.

[3] The total value of England's imports of iron, and of manufactures of cotton, wool, and flax, in 1856, *ten years* after the duties on them were repealed, was respectively as follows : —

Iron	£775,908
Manufactures of cotton	.664,001
,, ,, wool	1,444,162
,, ,, flax	97,541

' as we can see, was to admit raw materials free ; to diminish the cost of living by the free admission of corn
(breadstuffs), and thereby render the continuance of low
wages compatible with subsistence ; and to induce other
nations, if she could, to open their markets to the sale of
her productions. This constituted the sum and substance
of England's free-trade programme. I will now show how
this programme has been carried out, and the results it has
accomplished.

The Free-Trade Acts of England and their Effects.

The several tariff acts which comprise the principal free-
trade measures of England are as follows, viz.: The acts of
Sir Robert Peel in 1842 and 1845, his great act repealing the
corn laws in 1846, and the act of Mr. Gladstone in 1853.
The bearing which these acts severally had on the revenue,
and, inferentially, on the commerce of Great Britain, is
clearly shown by table A, which was compiled from her custom-house records. It gives the gross amount of customs
duties derived from each of the principal articles imported,
distinguishing the annual receipts in each of the years in
which the free-trade measures were respectively enacted, and
the mean annual receipts in a series of years before and after
each enactment. This record begins four years before the
first important measure of reform, and comes down six years
this side of its last important act. It shows that, from 1838
to 1859 inclusive, England derived over *ninety per cent* of
her customs revenue from sixteen articles, and that the
amount received from all other articles subject to duty was
less than *nine per cent*. The near approach to uniformity in
the sources, and the annual amount of revenue raised during
those twenty-two years, under the several free-trade acts, is
very remarkable.

TABLE A.

ARTICLES.	Mean Ann'l Amount collected in the Four Years from 1838 to 1841 inclusive.	Amount collected in 1842, the Year of Sir Robt. Peel's Tariff Reform.	Mean Ann'l Amount collected in the Years 1843 and 1844.	Mean Ann'l Amount collected in the Years 1845 and 1846, the Years of Sir Robt. Peel's great Tariff Reforms.	Mean Ann'l Amount collected in the Six Years from 1847 to 1852 inclusive.	Amount collected in 1853, the Year of Mr. Gladstone's Tariff Measures.	Mean Ann'l Amount collected in the Six Years from 1854 to 1859 inclusive.
	Dollars.¹	Dollars.	Dollars.	Dollars.	Dollars.	Dollars.	Dollars.
Butter	1,232,765	940,125	846,420	961,460	751,565	638,780	555,675
Cheese	596,270	497,220	520,515	577,910	446,535	298,315	240,215
Coffee	4,096,995	3,847,925	3,450,260	3,691,095	2,059,430	2,318,330	2,444,440
Corn (Breadstuffs)	3,814,570	6,891,310	4,675,440	2,011,575	2,343,600	2,063,455	2,352,673
Currants	980,130	1,143,525	1,371,135	1,317,245	1,554,335	733,535	1,100,165
Fruit, — Raw, Dried, and Preserved	1,135,450	1,183,415	1,325,585	1,382,385	1,346,310	1,306,180	1,098,905
Seeds	648,150	849,985	227,160	401,345	175,775	191,025	15,015
Silk, Manufactures of	1,214,800	1,085,995	1,320,590	1,397,100	1,042,920	1,377,070	1,405,430
Spirits	12,790,315	11,159,670	10,988,610	11,986,900	12,725,190	13,452,280	12,407,230
Sugar	24,331,385	24,424,160	25,784,375	18,973,755	20,600,900	20,521,680	27,280,580
Molasses	1,089,275	1,277,565	1,264,135	827,960	962,485	864,075	938,795
Tallow	946,265	855,325	923,885	693,585	413,990	448,720	346,770
Tea	18,095,740	20,447,635	22,332,245	24,863,235	27,705,730	28,430,965	26,071,440
Timber	7,885,765	4,875,395	4,049,495	5,429,510	3,311,110	2,897,240	2,921,545
Tobacco and Snuff	17,880,070	17,977,185	19,257,510	21,399,140	22,121,515	23,758,885	26,031,360
Wines	9,364,990	7,045,730	9,393,250	9,309,605	9,196,880	10,180,375	9,797,385
All other Articles subject to duty	10,542,715	8,485,900	8,908,110	4,231,435	3,235,270	2,962,755	2,770,060
Total	116,645,680	112,981,315	116,638,720	110,855,240	111,013,630	113,063,665	117,797,685
Percentage on the sixteen Articles specified	90.96	92.49	92.36	96.18	97.09	97.38	97.65
Percentage on all other Articles	9.04	7.51	7.64	3.82	2.91	2.62	2.35

¹ For the convenience of comparing English values with those of the United States, I have for this pamphlet converted pounds sterling into Federal currency at the rate of five dollars the pound.

In 1845, "by command of Her Majesty," an expository statement [1] was prepared and presented to Parliament, showing the effect of Peel's tariff act of 1842 on the imports of Great Britain, the imports being classified according to their relation to the questions of free trade and protection. The classification is as follows: —

ARTICLES IN A RAW STATE TO BE USED IN MANUFACTURE.
ARTICLES PARTIALLY MANUFACTURED.
ARTICLES WHOLLY MANUFACTURED.
ARTICLES FOR FOOD, INCLUDING CONDIMENTS AND STIMULANTS.
ARTICLES NOT PROPERLY BELONGING TO ANY OF THE FOREGOING HEADS.

A summary of the Expository Statement is given in

TABLE B.

CLASSES OF IMPORTS.	Mean Annual Amount of Duties collect'd in the Two Years *before* the Tariff of 1842.	Mean Annual Amount of Duties collect'd in the Two Years *after* the Tariff of 1842.	Excess collected in the Two Years *before* the Tariff of 1842.	Excess collected in the Two Years *after* the Tariff of 1842.
	Dollars.	Dollars.	Dollars.	Dollars.
Articles in a Raw State to be used in Manufactures . .	10,975,400	7,074,205	3,901,195	. . . . .
Articles partially manufact'd	5,256,145	3,257,440	1,998,705	. . . . .
Articles wholly manufactured	2,397,850	2,377,625	20,225	. . . . .
Articles for Food, &c. . . .	93,438,085	100,384,210	. . . . .	6,946,125
Articles not properly belonging to any of the foregoing heads	1,119,990	510,950	609,040	. . . . .
Total	113,187,470	113,604,430	6,529,165	6,946,125

By an examination of this table, it will be seen that the principal effect of the free-trade act of 1842, was to increase the total amount of duties collected, nearly *half a million dollars*, and to take about *six millions of dollars* from raw materials and articles partially manufactured, and add a similar amount to articles for food.

---

[1] Accounts and Papers of the British Parliament for the year 1845, vol. xlvi. pp. 100-287.

To show the bearing which the several free-trade acts —
viz., the acts of 1842, 1845, 1846, and 1853 — had *collectively*
on the same classes of imports, I present table C, which gives
the amount of duties collected on each class respectively, in
the year 1839, and in the year 1859.

TABLE C.

CLASSES OF IMPORTS.	Net Amount of Duty collected in the Year ending Jan. 5, 1839.	Net Amount of Duty collected in the Year ending Dec. 31, 1859.	Excess in 1839.	Excess in 1859.
	Dollars.	Dollars.	Dollars.	Dollars.
Articles in a Raw State to be used in Manufactures . .	10,519,115	1,528,395	8,990,720	. . . . . .
Articles partially manufact'd	5,220,795	2,076,495	3,144,300	. . . . . .
Articles wholly manufactured	2,396,260	3,032,575	. . . . . .	636,315
Articles for Food, &c. . . .	91,518,795	116,746,050	. . . . . .	25,227,255
Articles not properly belonging to any of the foregoing heads	949,795	139,120	810,675	. . . . . .
Total	110,604,760	123,522,635	12,945,695	25,863,570

From this table it appears that the combined effect of all
these free-trade acts up to 1859, was to increase the total annual
amount of duties collected, *twelve millions of dollars;* to increase the amount collected on articles wholly manufactured,
six hundred thousand dollars,[1] and on articles for food, *twenty-
five millions of dollars;* and to diminish the amount collected
on raw materials, nearly *nine millions of dollars;* and on
articles partially manufactured *three millions of dollars.*

The modifications which have been made in the British
tariff, since 1859, do not materially change its character, as
they relate mainly to the duties on the sixteen articles speci-
fied in Table A.

The greatest benefit which England has derived from her
tariff-reform measures, does not appear in the annual amount

---

[1] The duties on iron, and on manufactures of cotton, wool, and flax, were
repealed in 1846; but on manufactures of silk, paper, and leather, and on sundry
minor articles of manufacture, duties were retained till after 1859.

of her customs revenue, for that, as already shown, has been remarkably uniform. This benefit was largely prospective, and is to be seen in its relation to her imports of raw materials and of breadstuffs.

The amount of duties collected on raw materials to be used in manufacture, in 1839, was over *ten millions of dollars*.[1] The rates of duties that then prevailed, applied to the amount of raw materials now consumed in her vast manufacture, would amount annually to a very large sum. On cotton alone, it would amount to *eight millions of dollars*. Great Britain produces only forty per cent of the wheat and wheat-meal which she consumes.[2] In 1875, she imported corn (breadstuffs) to the value of *two hundred and sixty-five millions of dollars*.[3] Had the " sliding scale " of duties been continued, with corn at the prices which prevailed three years prior to its repeal, her bread-tax that year would have amounted to *fifty-three millions of dollars*.

But to understand fully the nature and necessity of the reform of Peel and Gladstone, we must take into view the fact that the details and provisions of the British tariff had become exceedingly numerous, complicated, and inconsistent. It contained many actual prohibitions, and many duties so high as to be, in fact, prohibitory. In the progress of manufactures and trade, not a few of its imposts had become entirely inoperative. It had grown up, as it were, by chance, to meet from time to time the exigencies of war and the demands of finance, until it had become a vast agglomeration of unintelligible impositions. Says Mr. Tooke : " The whole commercial system was incumbered, disfigured, and shackled by innumerable, vexatious, obstructive, and impolitic restrictions." To eliminate from such a mass what was positively injurious, or absolutely useless, and to simplify and to classify the whole, was a work of necessity and mercy, which, by

---

[1] See Table B, p. 14.

[2] See Twentieth Report of the Commissioners of Her Majesty's Customs, p. 10.

[3] See Twenty-third number, Statistical Abstract for the United Kingdom, p. 33.

relieving the custom-house, gave needed facilities to commerce. The common-sense act which erased from the statute-
book so many petty and annoying details, made no little
show of reform. Yet, so far as those details were concerned,
it had really no bearing on the great questions of free trade
and protection ; more than nine-tenths of the entire customs
receipts having been derived, as already shown, from sixteen
articles.

The facts I have adduced, show, I think, that in economic
and fiscal discussions, during the past thirty years, a greater
prominence has been given to the free-trade measures of
England than their results will justify. The influence of
these measures in extending British commerce has, also, been
much overestimated. It is true that, of late years, the
increase of British trade has been rapid and striking. But
causes of general application, which are to be found outside
of tariff laws, have contributed largely to this result. Prominent among those causes, are the influence of improved
machinery and of the applied sciences, and the greatly
increased supply of gold.

This is pre-eminently an age of progress. Useful inventions in the mechanic arts, and important discoveries in
science, are of almost daily occurrence. Countless improvements in existing machines, and in the methods and processes
of production, are continually enlarging the ability to produce, — multiplying articles of consumption, and thus, of
necessity, swelling the great currents of trade.

The annual produce of gold, which, prior to 1848, was
fifty millions of dollars, has, since 1853, amounted in some
years to *one hundred and fifty millions of dollars*. " The
effect of this triple supply of gold," says Mr. Tooke, " has
been to set in motion and sustain a vast and increasing number of causes, all conducing to augment the real wealth and
resources of the world, by stimulating trade, enterprise, discovery, and production." That the late increase of Great
Britain's trade is not due, in a controlling degree, to her
free-trade measures, is conclusively shown by the fact that
she is not alone in the enjoyment of an increasing commerce.

The foreign trade of Russia and of the United States increased, during the past ten years, under the policy of protection, in a greater ratio than that of Great Britain under the policy of free-trade ; and, also, in a greater ratio than that of France, which the English claim as a free-trade ally.

The following comparative Table, D, shows the percentage of increase (in round numbers) in the imports and the exports of merchandise of each of the countries just mentioned, during the ten years ending 1875 ; the mean amount of trade in 1866 and 1867, and the mean amount of trade in 1874 and 1875, being taken as the basis of computation.

TABLE D.

COUNTRIES COMPARED.	Increase in Imports.	Increase in Exports.
Russia [1]	104 per cent.	81 per cent.
United States [2]	33 „ „	72 „ „
Great Britain [1]	30 „ „	25 „ „
France [1]	13 „ „	16 „ „

Those who are accustomed so inconsiderately and flippantly to denounce our tariff as prohibitory and destructive of commerce would do well to ponder these facts.

THE TARIFF POLICY OF THE UNITED STATES, AND ITS RELATION TO THAT OF ENGLAND.

As the fitness of our tariff policy depends very much on the physical condition of the country, a glance at our indigenous resources, and at what we have done in the way of their development, may not be out of place.

. [1] See third number of England's Statistical Abstract, for the principal foreign countries, pp. 32–36.

[2] See Quarterly Report (No. 1) of the Chief of the Bureau of Statistics, p. 101. Our exceptionally large exports in 1874 and 1875, probably raised our percentage of increase above its normal rate.

Spanning the continent, with the Atlantic Ocean on one side and the almost boundless Pacific on the other, our Union spreads, and stretches its magnificent zone of more than twenty degrees in latitude and nearly three thousand miles in length. In extent of coast, whether of sea, lake, or gulf; in the number and value of harbors; and in the means of inland navigation, whether of sound, lake, or river, — what portion of the globe surpasses ours? An immense area of rich and varied soil, lying under a wide range of climate, enables us to raise in abundance and with certainty all the most valued products of the temperate zones. Besides the wealth of our vast and well-timbered forests, and all the teeming acres which are now under cultivation, we have yet in reserve a breadth of virgin soil sufficient to give employment and sustenance to many-fold our present population. Nor are our riches all on the surface. In mines and placers of gold, only one nation can compete with us. Of silver, copper, lead, zinc, and mercury, we have large supplies; while iron (more valuable than all the rest) is widely diffused, and inexhaustible in quantity. But it is in the almost incredible richness of our coal deposits — that mineral which has become so essential to individual comfort, to manufacturing success, to swift locomotion on land or water, to prosperity in peace, to efficiency in war, and, indeed, to all true national wealth and power — that we leave behind at an immeasurable distance every other nation. We have done much to use these gifts of Nature, and much, also, in preparation for their future utilization. We have deepened and protected the entrances to our harbors, and made our rivers more navigable. In number and length of railways, no country vies with ours. Mountain ranges of formidable height, and vast plains which once seemed of interminable length, are now traversed easily and quickly on the iron track. More quickly still, the telegraphic wire conveys over every part of our great republic the orders of government and the messages of business; so that parts of the country once widely separated in thought as well as space are now, for all purposes of intercourse, placed, as it were, side by side.

In manufacturing, we have made a fair start. Much of the raw material which we extract from the earth, or raise on its surface, — material which may be increased to any extent, — is converted, by skilful hands and labor-saving machinery, into forms and fabrics of utility and beauty. In the invention, the construction, and the use of mechanism, the Americans are allowed to show an aptness equal, at least, to that of other nations. Nowhere else is this faculty turned to more general or to more profitable account. Not only in manufacturing, but in agriculture and in almost every kind of industrial art, the employment of labor-saving machines and implements multiplies our numerical force, and vastly augments our productive power. The result is seen in the immense value of the annual productions of the United States, which now exceeds *six thousand millions of dollars*. That our industrial achievements and our present large producing power are in a great measure due to the varied industries which our tariff policy, vacillating as it has been, has rendered possible, no one, I think, who is familiar with the essential conditions of industrial progress will deny. The tariff acts of the United States have been numerous ; and, while revenue has been their primary object, they have also, for half a century, been framed with more or less regard to the protection of American industry. Their tariff policy, therefore, may be regarded, in the main, as a protective policy. As yet, however, we have failed to establish, in this important department of national economy, any policy of action so settled and uniform as to furnish our manufacturers with a safe basis of faith and practical dependence.

When our customs tariff again undergoes revision, it is to be hoped that Congress will adjust its provisions, not in conformity with the precepts of theorists, to whatever school of economists they may belong, but in conformity with our own needs and requirements. The aim should be to establish a *national* tariff policy, which shall be regarded as permanent, and so to frame its provisions as to promote the use and development of our vast national resources ; and to secure, so far as it depends on legislation, the highest attainable prosperity to all sections of the country. Obvious as this patriotic duty is, there are many among us, who, in disregard of national interests and requirements, would have us adopt England's tariff as our model ; and, illogical as it may seem, reproduce the same arguments for its adoption here that were used in England for its adoption there, under widely different circumstances. That we can learn much from her long and varied experience is no doubt true ; but to follow her example, except in so far as the conditions of the two countries are similar, would be unwise. Rightly to understand the relation which our tariff sustains to that of England, we must take into view the statistical facts contained in the following series of comparative tables : —

Table E shows the value of the import trade of the two countries, respectively, in the year 1875 ; the articles being classed in the manner adopted in the Expository Statement before mentioned.

TABLE E.

ARTICLES.	Great Britain[1] Imported	United States[2] Imported
	Dollars.	Dollars.
Articles in a Raw State to be used in Manufacture . . .	695,237,440	68,260,780
Articles partially manufactured	142,841,330	35,124,760
Articles wholly manufactured .	197,760,880	197,175,421
Articles for Food, including condiments and stimulants . .	811,374,750	208,345,178
Articles not properly belonging to any of the foregoing heads	22,483,485	38,143,978
Total	1,869,697,885	517,050,117

[1] See Twentieth Report of the Commissioners of her Majesty's Customs, p. 29.

[2] The figures in this column were compiled from the Report of the Chief of the Bureau of Statistics on Commerce and Navigation, for 1875. I desire here to express my thanks to Dr. Edward Young, for his courtesy in sending me that Report, and other official documents which I have used in the preparation of this work.

The amount of revenue which each country respectively derived from customs duties, and from internal taxes, in the year 1875, is given in

TABLE F.

BRANCHES OF REVENUE.	Great Britain.	United States.
	Dollars.	Dollars.
Derived from Customs Duties .	100,027,165	154,551,982
Internal Taxes	189,009,305	110,545,154
Total	289,036,470	265,100,136

Table G shows the classes of articles from which the two countries, respectively, derived their customs revenue ; the articles being classed as in Table E.

TABLE G.

ARTICLES.	Great Britain.[1]	United States.[2]
	Dollars.	Dollars.
Derived from Articles in a Raw State, to be used in Manf'ure	. . . . . .	6,478,324
Articles partially manufactured	. . . . . .	4,819,495
Articles wholly manufactured .	. . . . . .	82,168,214
Articles for Food, including condiments and stimulants . .	100,027,165	57,294,462
Articles not properly belonging to any of the foregoing heads	. . . . . .	3,794,487
Total	100,027,165	154,554,982

The sources from which each country derived its internal revenue is shown in Table H.

---

[1] See Twentieth Report of the Commissioners of her Majesty's Customs, p. 98.

[2] The figures in this column were compiled from the Report of the Chief of the Bureau of Statistics on Commerce and Navigation, for 1875.

TABLE H.

SOURCES.	Great Britain.[1]	United States.[2]
	Dollars.	Dollars.
Derived from Spirits	74,478,840	52,081,091
Malt and Fermented Liquors .	38,733,700	9,144,004
Tobacco	. . . . . .	37,303,461
Stamps	52,738,645	6,557,229
Licenses	17,498,780	. . . . . .
Banks and Bankers	. . . . . .	4,097,248
Other sources	5,550,340	1,361,221
Total	189,009,305	110,545,151

We have now before us the value of the imports of Great Britain and of the United States, in 1875, classified according to their bearing on the questions of free-trade and protection; the amount of revenue which each country raised by customs duties and by internal taxes; and the articles and sources from which each branch of revenue was respectively derived. In the light of these and other facts already adduced, I will endeavor to show wherein we can, and wherein we cannot, wisely conform our tariff to that of England.

IMPORTS OF THE TWO COUNTRIES. — From Table E, p. 21, it appears that, in 1875, Great Britain imported merchandise to the value of *one thousand eight hundred and sixty-nine million dollars;* and the United States, to the value of only *five hundred and forty-seven million dollars.*

The greater value of the foreign trade of Great Britain is thought by many to place her in a position of relative advantage. On the contrary, it is the result of a position of relative disadvantage. Nations are independent and prosperous in proportion as they have within themselves the means of subsistence. In this view, Great Britain is the most dependent, and the United States the most independent, of all the great nations of the earth. For us, foreign trade is certainly

---

[1] See Statistical Abstract for the United Kingdom, 23d number, p. 9.
[2] See Report of the Commissioner of Internal Revenue, 1876, p. 169.

desirable, so far as it results from national growth and development; but, for Great Britain, it is an absolute necessity. To subsist her population, she must annually import articles for food to the value of over *eight hundred million dollars;* and, to pay for these articles, she must also import raw materials to be used in manufacture to the value of nearly *seven hundred million dollars*, and annually sell her manufactured productions in foreign markets to the value of *twelve hundred million dollars*. Does any American covet a foreign trade resting on a basis of such international dependence? To maintain that commercial regulations, which are suited to the needs of dependent Britain, are alike applicable to independent America, is the height of absurdity.

REVENUE OF THE TWO COUNTRIES. — Table F, p. 22, shows that the amount of revenue which Great Britain derived in 1875 from customs duties and internal taxes was *two hundred and eighty-nine million dollars*, and that the amount which the United States derived from those branches was *two hundred and sixty-five millions of dollars;* and that, while our customs revenue was *fifty-four millions of dollars* more than that of Great Britain, our internal revenue was *seventy-eight millions of dollars* less. But, from both branches together, she raised *twenty-four millions of dollars* more than we did.

By an examination of Tables G and H, p. 22, 23, considerable disparity will be seen to exist in the articles and sources from which the two countries respectively derive their customs and their internal revenue. In all that has been said in advocacy of our adopting England's customs tariff, her internal tax laws are rarely mentioned. There is no more reason why we should unqualifiedly adopt the one than the other.

To show more fully the relation which our tariff sustains to that of England, I will now present the subject in conformity with the classification of imports in the expository statement before explained; beginning, for convenience, with

DUTIES ON ARTICLES FOR FOOD. — It is a noticeable fact, that the whole of the revenue which Great Britain derives from customs, and sixty per cent of that which she derives from excise, is a tax on articles for food. As to the bearing which such a tax has on the people, the Commissioners of her Majesty's Customs, in their Twentieth Report, say, " It has always been held by the best authorities on questions relating to the incidence of taxation, that the bulk of the revenue from customs, of which almost the whole is derived from tobacco, spirits, tea, dried fruit, coffee, and cocoa, is paid by that class of the population which is dependent upon weekly wages, — comprising, as it does, the great majority ; for wine, consumed principally by a richer class, contributes less than nine per cent of the whole." What the commissioners say in regard to the effect on the people of customs duties on articles for food, is also true in regard to excise duties on these articles. Therefore, of the taxes, nine-tenths of which are paid by that class of the population which is dependent upon weekly wages, Great Britain raises *two hundred and thirteen million dollars*, and the United States only *one hundred and fifty-five million dollars ;* that is to say, she raises *fifty-eight million dollars* more than we do. So far, then, as it relates to articles for food, the English revenue system contains nothing which suggests any improvement in our own.

DUTIES ON RAW MATERIALS. — Again recurring to Table E, p. 21, it will be seen that, in 1875, Great Britain imported raw materials to be used in manufacture to the value of *six hundred and ninety-five million dollars*, and the United States to the value of only *sixty-eight million dollars ;* the excess in favor of Great Britain being *six hundred and twenty-seven million dollars.* As already shown, the English tariff admits this class of articles free of duty. Although our tariff has a large free list, — larger, I think, than is generally supposed, — it imposes on certain raw materials duties, which, in 1875, amounted in the aggregate to *six million four hundred and seventy-eight thousand dollars.*

The expediency of a nation imposing customs duties on raw materials depends largely on the sources of its prosperity. For England, whose indigenous resources are limited, and whose prosperity is largely dependent on manufacturing from imported raw materials, to impose customs duties on those raw materials would be an act of folly. With the United States, the case is quite different. Their indigenous resources are almost boundless, and their highest prosperity is to be derived from the utilization of these resources. In accomplishing this result, if customs duties are necessary to enable their producers of raw materials to compete successfully with similar producers in other countries, it is wise policy to impose them.

The framers of our present tariff seem to have acted on that principle. Such raw materials as do not compete with home industry are admitted free of duty ; and on such as do so compete, and are of national importance, duties are imposed. Feeble but persevering efforts are made by some writers to spread the idea, that our manufacturers are oppressed by duties on their raw materials.

I have just shown that the total amount of duties we collected in 1875, on all our imports of raw materials to be used in manufacture, was, in round numbers, only *six million four hundred and seventy-eight thousand dollars.* Of this sum, *three million seven hundred and ninety thousand dollars* came from duties on wool, leaving but *two million six hundred and eighty-eight thousand dollars* bearing on other manufactures. As the total annual value of our manufactures of wool, including worsteds and carpets, exceeds *one hundred and ninety-nine million of dollars*, it will be seen that the duties on the wool used amount to scarcely *two per cent* on the value of the manufactured product. The duties on other raw materials than wool bear a *still less average percentage* to the aggregate value of the various manufactures to which they directly or indirectly relate.

Our present tariff on wool and manufactures of wool places the wool manufacturer, so far as his relation to foreign competitors is concerned, on the same footing as though he received his wool free of duty. On manufactures of wool it imposes a specific duty, equivalent to the amount of the duty on the wool entering into such manufactures. It then adds a duty for revenue and protection the same as is imposed on manufactures of cotton and of iron, on the raw material of which no duty is needed or imposed. It cannot be justly said, therefore, that the duty on wool oppresses the wool manufacturer. This system of adjusting the duties on manufactures of wool relatively to the duties on wool is a marked feature of the present tariff. It allows of equal protection being given to the wool grower and the wool manufacturer; and under its operation the wool industry of the country, in all its branches, has been largely developed.

The duties on wool are justified by considerations of public policy. Sheep husbandry is essential to industrial as well as national independence. Every civilized and semi-civilized nation has its flocks. The whole number of sheep in the world is estimated at *four hundred and eighty-four million.* Of this number, Great Britain has *thirty-four million,* and the United States about the same number. Sheep husbandry benefits a nation by fertilizing its soil, by furnishing a necessary fibre for clothing its people, and, above all, by contributing to its supply of animal food. In populous regions, the mutton of a sheep is much more valuable than its wool. The value of the produce of sheep husbandry in Great Britain is stated, on good authority, to amount annually to *one hundred and fifty-nine millions of dollars;* over *one hundred million dollars* of this sum being derived from the mutton. The value of the produce of sheep husbandry in the United States, I have not seen stated. It is known, however, that our domestic fleeces supply *ninety per cent* of the wool used in our extensive woollen goods manufacture; the value of which, in 1870, exceeded *one hundred and fifty-five million dollars.* There are ways in which the United States are or may be peculiarly benefited by sheep husbandry. But, as I have not the space to present them, I will refer my readers to a very able discussion of the subject by Mr. John L. Hayes, in an article entitled "The Part of the Wool Industry in our National Economy."[1]

---

[1] See Bulletin of the National Association of Wool Manufacturers, vol. vi. pp. 221-253.

The question is sometimes asked, why sheep husbandry in
the United States, with low-priced land, requires a duty on
wool to sustain it; when, in England, with relatively high-
priced land, it prospers without a duty. To this question there are several answers. I have space to mention
only one or two of them. The sheep which are now
mostly grown in England are the " mutton sheep ;" such as
the Southdowns, the Cotswold, and the Leicester. These
breeds of sheep not only yield a large amount of animal food,
but produce a long-stapled wool, which is of special value in
the manufacture of worsted goods. In the textile industry
of England, the worsted manufacture is second only to that of
cotton. It has grown up with English sheep husbandry in
such relations of reciprocal dependence, that the raising of
worsted wools and the manufacture of them have acted and
reacted on each other, and developed a distinctive national
industry. Such worsted wools as England produces are in
limited supply the world over. British farmers and writers
declare that " the sheep is literally the basis of English
husbandry ; that they have become an indispensable necessity,
as there is no other means of keeping up the land." [1] Now,
if we take into view its benefit to her agriculture, the value
of its mutton, and the fact that only a comparatively small
amount of competing wools are grown elsewhere, we
readily see how England's sheep husbandry can prosper
without the encouragement of law. In the United States,
the conditions relating to sheep husbandry are quite different
from those in England.

Notwithstanding that the raising of long-wool sheep has
made considerable progress here under our present tariff, the
sheep mostly grown in this country are of the merino type.
The wools they produce, having a wide range of uses, have
to compete with the wools of Australia, the Argentine Republic, and other wool-producing countries. As our merino
sheep, in greater part, are raised in large flocks, in sparsely

---

[1] Bulletin of the National Association of Wool Manufacturers, vol. vi.
p. 153.

populated parts of the country, the mutton — which, in England, is the most valuable part of sheep husbandry — cannot, generally speaking, be turned to very much account. Much more might be said in answer to the above interrogatory, but the facts already stated are enough to show that the question of duties or no duties on wool is a very different one in the United States from what it is in England. Again, it may be asked, why our farmers have not raised more of the long-wool sheep. Prominent among the causes which have retarded the extension of this important branch of sheep husbandry, is bad tariff legislation. The tariff of 1846, which put a horizontal duty on wool and manufactures of wool, was hostile both to wool growing and wool manufacturing; and the consequence was that the wool manufacture was prostrated, and sheep husbandry languished for the want of a market for its wool. Under such a tariff, the worsted manufacture could get no foothold here. It was not until after the adoption of the system of wool duties before explained, that it took root. Under that system, the worsted manufacture has made rapid strides, and now annually exceeds in value *twenty millions of dollars.* Consequent upon the demand for worsted wool created by the development of the worsted manufacture, the raising of the long-wool, mutton sheep has been nationalized, and is being extended.

DUTIES ON ARTICLES PARTIALLY MANUFACTURED. — England, in 1875, as shown by Table E, p. 21, imported articles partially manufactured to the value of *one hundred and forty-two million dollars,* and the United States to the value of only *thirty-five million dollars.* On our imports of this class of articles we impose an average duty of about *fourteen per cent,* amounting in the aggregate to *four million eight hundred and nineteen thousand dollars.* In England, they are admitted duty free. The reasons for our imposing duties on articles partially manufactured are substantially the same as those which justify duties on raw materials; and, as those reasons have already been stated, they need not be repeated here.

DUTIES ON ARTICLES WHOLLY MANUFACTURED. — In 1875, as shown by the table just referred to, England imported articles wholly manufactured, to the value of *one hundred and ninety-seven million dollars ;* and the United States, to about the same value.   From their imports of this class of articles, the United States derived *eighty-two million dollars* of customs revenue, and England derived *none.*

I have already shown how largely England depended on the protection of law to develop her resources and to establish her manufactures.   I have also pointed out the exigencies which compelled her to reverse her tariff policy.   That her tariff measures in the main have been well suited to her needs, I do not deny.   But, however expedient the repeal of her duties on manufactures may have seemed at the time it was done, it is now a question whether it has not proved detrimental to her.[1]   It is true that, for some time after the repeal of these duties her imports of manufactures (excepting those of silk) did not much increase ; but, in later years, manufacture has made such rapid progress in other countries that England now encounters a strong foreign competition.

In 1875, *one hundred and ninety-seven million dollars'* worth of articles wholly manufactured, and *one hundred and forty-two million dollars'* worth of articles partially manufactured, were thrown upon her home market.   The admission of raw materials free, and of corn (breadstuffs) at a nominal duty, was the only feature of her free-trade measures that

---

[1] A cry which seemed to be dead has therefore suddenly revived, — the cry for protection, although it is at present but faintly heard.   There are sometimes little "news paragraphs" in the daily journals which are better worth attention than the leading articles ; and perhaps some of our readers noticed a few days ago a few lines setting forth that a deputation of English silk manufacturers had waited upon Lord Derby requesting him to get a reduction of French duties on our silk, or else to lay heavy duties on French silks brought over here.   Protection seemed as extinct as the Wars of the Roses, but here it is again ; and, what is more, we venture to predict that we shall see a good deal more of it during the next few years than many people suppose.   " We must think only of the consumers," the working-men are told.   But when the producers are nearly as numerous as the consumers, and find themselves on the verge of starvation, what they will demand remains to be seen. — *London World.*

strengthened her position against foreign competition. The repeal of the duties on manufactures could have no such effect ; and, had these duties been retained, her exports would not have been diminished, and her home market would have remained unimpaired. But, rightly to understand the grounds of England's policy in this regard, we must keep in view the fact, that to induce other nations to relax their commercial regulations was and is her constant aim, — an aim which largely sways her diplomatic as well as her legislative action. For several years *before* the enactment of her free-trade measures, the whole influence of the government, with all the aid diplomacy could render, was exerted to induce the nations with which England deals to favor, by commercial treaties, the admission of her productions. These efforts were in every case *unsuccessful.*[1] Neither the profound arguments of Downing Street, nor the persuasiveness of able and wily embassadors, could bring those nations to believe that it would be better for them to allow Great Britain to do their manufacturing. When this great and disinterested instructor of the nations had exhausted every other method in vain endeavors to convince them that she understood their interests far better than they themselves understood them, she resolved to make one more effort ; namely, that of teaching by example. To this end she adopted "free-trade" as her *watchword*, and enacted the so-called free-trade measures, the character and effects of which I have already explained. The duties on manufactures which these measures repealed had become an insignificant item in the receipts of the custom-house. At the time of their repeal, the total annual amount of duties collected on iron, and on manufactures of cotton, wool, and flax, was less than *half a million dollars*. Had England regarded the repeal of these duties with sole reference to her domestic interests, it is not likely that it would have occurred ; for it must have been obvious that its effect would be to weaken rather than strengthen her home market. But her object was to enlarge her foreign market. By setting an example

---

[1] See Mr. Gladstone's letter to Mr. Hadfield, p. 47.

in the direction of free-trade, she hoped to induce other nations to relax their tariffs, and thereby increase the foreign demand for her productions in a greater ratio than the home demand diminished under open competition. Her anticipations in this regard, however, have not been realized. The figures which I have already given show that, since the repeal of these duties, she has lost no inconsiderable part of her home market; and there is no evidence that by that repeal she has gained an equivalent foreign market. In adopting this policy, England no doubt reckoned on being able to maintain her pre-eminence as a manufacturing nation; and probably would have done so, had other nations acted on her free-trade advice, and allowed the importation of British productions to dwarf their own manufacturing industry. But those nations — choosing to imitate England's earlier practice, rather than follow her later advice — continued to defend their own industries; and now, instead of being her industrial dependents, are her formidable rivals.

In no other country does England watch the course of tariff legislation, or strive so much to influence it, as in the United States; and for obvious reasons. Of all the foreign markets for her productions, ours is the largest. According to the report of the " Bureau of Statistics," our imports from Great Britain, during the ten years ending 1876, amounted in value to *one thousand eight hundred and thirteen million dollars*. In the year 1872, the value of our imports from that source was *two hundred and forty-nine million dollars*,[1] and their mean annual value for the ten years in question was *one hundred and eighty-one million dollars*. Nearly *three-fourths* of these imports were productions of the United Kingdom, and consisted mainly of manufactures. These large importations, be it remembered, took place under our present tariff, which is not unfrequently stigmatized as a prohibitory tariff. A tariff which allows over *one hundred and thirty-five million dollars'* worth of manufactures to be annually thrown upon our market, from one country alone, is very far from being prohibitory. It must be obvious to all who will look at the facts,

---

[1] Quarterly Report (No. 1) of the Bureau of Statistics for 1877, p. 91.

and can trace causes to their effects, that had our duties been materially lower than they are, excessive importation would have prostrated our manufacturing industry. Nevertheless, there are many among us who, in disregard of facts, contend that our customs duties retard the development of our manufactures, and that under free-trade we should be better able to withstand foreign competition than we now are. This is a position which they assume without giving the slightest proof in support of it. Fortunately, we are not left to theory alone for a decision of this question. We have a practical demonstration of it based upon actual experience. The history of the silk manufacture of England conclusively shows what the condition of our manufacturing industry generally would be if our customs duties were repealed. At one time, the silk manufacture was the third in value of Great Britain's textile industries. In 1860, it amounted (in round numbers) to *ninety-four million dollars*. Of this amount, *seventy-nine million dollars*' worth entered into home consumption, and *fifteen million dollars*' worth were exported.[1] This important branch of industry owed its origin and development in Great Britain to prohibitory or high protective duties. In 1824, the duties were reduced to *thirty per cent ad valorem*. They were afterwards further reduced. Mr. Gladstone, in 1853, in his Budget speech of that year, spoke in regard to them as follows : " We have not thought it right to propose a reduction in the silk duties, which are *fifteen* per cent; the question of the silk-duties is mainly a question of revenue, and in regard to it we do not think it is an article that has the strongest claims upon our consideration ; for, so far as it is an article into the manufacture of which protection enters, the protection has mainly reference to certain classes of operatives, with respect to whom it would be the disposition of Parliament to proceed carefully and with great circumspection."

Notwithstanding that Mr. Gladstone, speaking as Prime Minister of England, virtually admitted that " certain classes of operatives " (meaning the silk operatives) needed protection, the industry which gave them their means of sub-

---

[1] London Journal of the Society of Arts, vol. ix. No. 433.

sistence was finally sacrificed in behalf of England's one great aim, namely, to command the foreign markets of the world. For England, while professing free-trade, and advising other nations to adopt it, to maintain protective duties on the only branch of her industry which, at that time, needed them, was an inconsistency which impeached her sincerity, and weakened her free-trade influence abroad. Under the pressure of these circumstances, her silk duties, in 1860, were repealed. The removal of these duties brought disaster to the silk industry of England. Her home market was flooded with foreign silks, numerous manufacturers of silk failed, thousands of silk operatives were thrown out of employment, and that once prosperous industry was largely prostrated. The enormous extent to which foreign silks were thrown upon her home market, after the repeal of the duties, is shown in Table I., which gives the value of the imports of silk manufactures into Great Britain, in each year, from 1854 to 1875: —

TABLE I.

Years.	Value of Imports.[1]	Years.	Value of Imports.
	Dollars.		Dollars.
1854	11,550,855	1865	41,677,235
1855	11,994,365	1866	46,563,090
1856	13,263,965	1867	44,922,375
1857	11,827,075	1868	53,977,260
1858	11,085,535	1869	58,973,800
1859	11,345,860	1870	75,491,635
1860 [2]	16,718,805	1871	40,978,625
1861	28,647,225	1872	45,709,315
1862	31,992,810	1873	48,902,445
1863	32,209,745	1874	58,710,330
1864	37,409,035	1875	60,091,660

I invite a careful examination of this instructive table. It shows that, from 1859 to 1861, — that is, the year before and the year after the repeal of the silk duties, — the im-

---

[1] The figures in this Table for 1854 to 1860 were derived from the "Annual Statement of the Trade and Navigation of the United Kingdom;" and for 1861 and the following years, from "Statistical Abstract for the United Kingdom," 23d Number, pp. 36, 37.

[2] In 1860 the duties on manufactures of silk were repealed.

ports of silk manufactures into Great Britain increased *one hundred and fifty per cent;* and that from 1859 to 1875, the increase was *five hundred per cent.* Thus it appears that the value of foreign silk manufactures put upon the home market, in displacement of English silk manufactures, was *forty-eight million dollars* more in 1875 than in 1859.

In view of these facts, it is not surprising to find the silk manufacturers of England asking for protection.[1]

To understand fully the relation which the tariff experience of England in regard to her silk industry has to our own tariff policy, we must take into view the fact, that the silk industry of England sustains a relation to foreign competition similar to that which our manufacturing industries generally sustain. There are conditions of production which enable the silk manufacturers of the Continent of Europe to undersell the silk manufacturers of England; and there are conditions of production (as I shall show hereafter) which enable the manufacturers of England and of the Continent to undersell our manufacturers. For these reasons, neither the silk industry of England nor the manufacturing industries of the United States can prosper without protective duties.

The disparities in the conditions of production which exist between England and the Continent are very much less than those which exist between the United States and England and the Continent. England's duty of fifteen per cent as effectually protected her silk industry as our present tariff protects our manufacturing industries. England has tried the experiment of repealing her silk duties, the disastrous results of which I have already set forth. Shall we repeat the blunder, by repealing our duties on manufactures generally? If England's repeal of her silk duties prostrated her silk industry, can any one doubt that the repeal of our duties on manufactures would prostrate our manufacturing industries?

I have dwelt long on the experience of England in regard to her silk duties, as it furnishes the most decisive proof of the unsoundness of the views of those who assert that our

---

[1] See citation from the " London World," at the foot of page 30.

manufacturing industries would prosper better under the policy of free-trade than under the policy of protection.

The question is often asked, Why are protective duties required to develop and sustain manufactures in the United States? Not, certainly, because our countrymen are less capable than their European rivals; for, in intelligence, ingenuity, and aptness to learn, they have no superiors. It is not because our natural advantages are less, nor from inability to acquire the requisite skill; for we have carried some manufactures to a perfection nowhere else attained. There are, however, certain conditions which affect, directly or indirectly, the cost of production, in respect of which other manufacturing nations have a decided advantage over us. Prominent among these disadvantageous conditions, though not all of them, are the rates of interest on capital, the rates of wages paid for labor, and the rates of local taxation. That these are things beyond the control of our manufactures, no one will deny. That the necessity of paying, in all these respects, much higher rates than their rivals have to pay, puts them at a serious disadvantage, seems equally certain. Let us see how this case stands. For the fifteen years ending 1860, the rate of interest in England averaged 4.02 per cent; in France, 4.16 per cent; and in the United States, 9.12 per cent, — showing a disparity against us of *five* per cent.[1]

---

[1] *Statement of the Comparative Rates of Interest in England, France, and the United States, in each Year, from 1846 to 1860.*

YEARS.	ENGLAND.		BANK OF FRANCE.	UNITED STATES.
	MARKET.	BANK.		
	Per cent.	Per cent.	Per cent.	Per cent.
1846	3.79	3.21	4.00	8.35
1847	5.85	5.21	4.92	9.54
1848	3.21	3.71	4.00	15.12
1849	2.31	2.94	4.00	10.08 -
1850	2.25	2.52	4.00	8.02
1851	3.06	3.00	4.00	9 68
1852	1.91	2.15	3.21	6.42
1853	3.67	3.69	3.21	10.21
1854	4.94	5.31	4.33	10.37
1855	4.67	5.64	4.42	8.96
1856	5.90	5.90	5.54	8.92
1857	6 69	6.59	6.00	12.77
1858	3.15	3.23	3.67	4.99
1859	2.74	2.74	3.46	6.59
1860	4.42	4.42	3 67	6.80
Mean rate for the 15 years	3.90	4.02	4.16	9.12

At the present time, the rate of interest is exceptionally low in all commercial countries. There is no reason to suppose, however, that, with a revival of business, the normal rates will not return. Therefore, taking all these facts into account, I think it is safe to say that in the long run the average rate of interest is twice as high here as it is with our principal foreign competitors; and that this disparity against us is at least *three* per cent. In England, a manufacturer is taxed only on the rental value of his buildings; whereas here the whole amount of his capital employed is taxed, and to an extent which makes the disparity against him fully *one* per cent. Skilled labor is well paid in all manufacturing countries, and commands about the same wages elsewhere as here; but our wages for common labor, which makes up the principal part of the pay-roll, are *twenty-five* per cent higher.[1] But for these and other inequalities of condition, our manufacturers could enter the race of competition with little fear of being distanced by any foreign rival. It is mainly upon this ground that they need protective duties. They seek no monopoly, no exclusive privilege. Give them an even chance in the game, and they will take care of themselves. But not until the cost of labor, taxation, and capital, through a gradual approximation, or by some great alteration here or there, shall have become nearly the same in Europe and America, will it be safe to abandon our present tariff policy. So long as local

---

[1] Mr. David A. Wells, when Special Commissioner of Revenue, investigated this subject at home and abroad, and thus states the difference between the rates of wages paid in the United States and the rates which obtain in several other countries, gold being taken as the standard in all cases: —

In the cotton manufacture, the excess of wages paid in the United States over the wages paid in Great Britain is 27 7-10 per cent; over Belgium, the excess is 48 per cent.

In the wool manufacture, the excess over Great Britain is, in woollen mills, 25 per cent; in carpet and worsted mills, 58 per cent. Over France, Belgium, Prussia, and Austria, the average excess is 100 per cent.

In iron foundries and machinery building, the excess over British wages is 58 per cent.

In the manufacture of iron, the average weekly wages paid to puddlers (in gold) are $16.24 in the United States; $8.75 in England; $8 in France; $6 in Belgium; $1.39 in Russia. — *Report for the Year* 1868.

taxation shall depend on the will and action of the several States, so long as the rates of wages and of interest in our country are kept up by the abundance of land and the demand for labor, neither skill nor assiduity on the part of our producers can remove the causes of that disparity which places them at so great disadvantage. The remedy, the only remedy, is in the hands of our national government. With that power it rests to say whether, in this great question of public and economic policy, their own people or foreigners shall be first considered.

OUR EXPORTS OF MANUFACTURES.

For nearly half a century, we have annually exported more or less of domestic manufactures. At first, these exports were small in amount; and, although they have increased with the growth of the country, the relative progress which we have made does not enable us to look with much confidence to that line of trade as a rapidly increasing source of national prosperity. From a quarter supposed to be well informed upon the subject, delusive statements have been put forth in regard to our ability to compete with other manufacturing nations in neutral markets. A wide publicity has been given to these statements, and short paragraphs of the same tenor often appear in the daily papers. The main drift of these publications is to the effect that the United States can now, as a *general* fact, manufacture. at less cost than other manufacturing nations; and that a growing foreign demand for her manufactures will open to her in the immediate future a career of prosperity hitherto unknown. The time may come when these pleasing anticipations may be realized; but in the nature of things it must be at some far distant day. From the circumstance of our being able to export certain articles of domestic manufacture, the inference has been inconsiderately drawn that, as a *general* fact, we surpass in cheapness of production all other countries. A broader view of the question does not justify such an inference. I have already shown that the disparities against us in the rates of interest, wages, and local taxation, inevitably, as a *general* fact, make the cost of manufacturing here greater than it is abroad. The general expenses of carrying on business are also much greater here than with our foreign rivals; and, though the difference cannot be expressed in figures, it is known to be such as materially to enhance the cost of production.

A nation that manufactures at relative disadvantage will always be able to export more or less of its productions. Improvements in machinery, a new article of manufacture, indigenous raw materials, or a peculiar condition of markets and of exchanges, may at times, and in special cases, counterbalance the general disadvantage, and induce an exceptional export trade. By looking over the official list of our exports of manufactures, any person acquainted with the conditions of production will see that they are, for the most part, exceptional, and that there are special reasons why we are able to export them. We export bark-tanned leather, because the bark used costs here less than one-half of what it costs abroad, although the labor of tanning costs more. We export fire-arms, by reason of improved machinery and the practice of the interchangeable system of parts, whereby a given part of one arm will fit any similar arm, — an advantage which gives the American arms the preference, at higher cost, over the arms made abroad, where that system has not been adopted. We export sewing-machines, because they are of American origin; but, since their manufacture has been established in other countries, the number of machines exported has greatly fallen off. American sewing-silk has been exported, not, however, because we can manufacture sewing-silk at less cost than other countries, — for the reverse of that is true, — but because it was adapted to machine use, and consequently followed the American sewing-machine abroad. Our earliest exports of cotton goods were mainly to China; and consisted, for the most part, of an article known as " brown drilling," — a fabric of American origin. At first, it met with no foreign competition; and, being well suited to the needs of the Chinaman, it got a foothold in that market, which it has maintained to this day. In later years the cotton fabrics which we export have been considerably diversified, and the markets to which they are sent have been multiplied; nevertheless, the value of the trade has not much increased. In 1860, the total value (in round numbers) of our exports of cotton manufactures was *ten million and nine hundred thousand dollars ;* and, for the fiscal year just closed, it was *twelve million and eighty-eight thousand dollars,* — a gain of only *eleven hundred and eighty-eight thousand dollars* in seventeen years.[1] In this brief history of our exports of domestic manufactures, I see no evidence that, as a *general* fact, we manufacture at less cost than other nations. If we could do so in respect of any of the great industries, it would be that of the cotton manufacture ; for the raw material is indigenous, and we have the best of machinery, large associated capitals, ample skill, and persevering enterprise employed in it. Yet, in 1875, while we exported cotton manufactures to the value of only *nine hundred and eighteen thousand dollars,* we imported them to the value of *twenty-seven million dollars,* and paid thereon the present duties. Now, if we can manufacture at less cost than other nations, why did our cotton manufacturers curtail their production, and in 1875 allow foreign cotton manufactures to the value of *twenty-seven million dollars,* paying an average duty of *thirty-three per cent,* to be thrown upon their home market ?

The growth of our exports of cotton manufactures, as compared with that of Great Britain, during the past thirty years, forbids the belief that we are to have a rapid increase of trade in that line.

Table J shows the value of the cotton manufactures exported by the United States and by Great Britain, in each year from 1846 to 1875, and by the United States to 1877.

---

[1] Exceptional circumstances attended the exports of the year just closed. The prices of cotton goods were unusually low in *currency ;* and by sending them out of the country the exporter got the advantage of the premium on gold, and, to the extent of the exports, relieved the glut in the home market. Moreover, special efforts were made to increase that trade, and tentative ventures were made, the results of which have not transpired. Of these exports, $1,852,622 worth were sent to Canada.

TABLE J.

YEARS.	United States Exported.	Great Britain Exported.
	Dollars.	Dollars.
1846	3,545,481	127,999,130
1847	4,082,523	116,666,125
1848	5,718,205	113,400,000
1849	4,933,129	133,875,675
1850	4,734,424	141,282,005
1851	7,241,205	150,444,180
1852	7,672,151	149,390,435
1853	8,768,894	163,564,510
1854	5,750,335	158,729,285
1855	5,857,181	173,895,705
1856	6,967,309	191,163,705
1857	6,115,177	195,367,100
1858	5,651,504	215,006,610
1859	8,316,222	241,011,125
1860	10,934,796	260,061,900
1861	7,957,038	234,362,445
1862	2,946,464	183,754,855
1863	2,906,411	237,985,940
1864	1,930,573	274,411,645
1865	876,702	286,330,605
1866	361,874	373,065,230
1867	389,653	354,184,915
1868	906,195	338,433,800
1869	531,745	335,584,870
1870	921,110	357,081,725
1871	1,680,951	364,107,055
1872	1,365,885	400,820,775
1873	1,436,068	386,815,060
1874	1,218,092	371,238,135
1875	918,813	358,858,565
1876	1,593,285	. . . . .
1877	12,088,465	. . . . .

From this table it appears that, in 1875, — the latest year for which I have the English returns, — the United States exported cotton manufactures to the value of *nine hundred and eighteen thousand dollars*, and Great Britain to the value of *three hundred and fifty-eight million eight hundred thousand dollars ;* that is, she exported *three hundred and ninety* times as much as we did.

I would invite all who are accustomed to assert that we beat Great Britain in the manufacture of cotton, and can drive her out of neutral markets, to ponder well the comparative figures in this table, and answer this question : At the relative rate of progress of the two countries, indicated by the table, how long will it take the United States to get so far ahead of Great Britain as to justify their assertions ?

Of kindred origin, and alike delusive, is the idea, that under free-trade our exports of domestic manufactures would increase. The adoption of that policy at our present stage of progress would diminish, rather than increase, such exports. Under free-trade, the law of demand and supply would bring the prices of commodities here to a general level with prices abroad ; whereas, there are conditions that affect the cost of production which do not obey that law. We have always had free-trade in capital and in labor, and yet the rate of interest and the rate of wages (as I have already shown) rule much higher here than in older countries. Were we to adopt free-trade, the disparities against us in the cost of general expenses, in the rate of interest, and in the rate of local taxation, would remain unchanged ; and, though the rate of wages might be somewhat reduced, our abundance of land would prevent its falling to the English and Continental rates. Free-trade, therefore, would reduce the prices of manufactured articles here in a greater ratio than it reduced the cost of their production, and thus open our market to a foreign competition which would take the life and energy out of our manufacturing industry, retard its progress, and thereby weaken our ability to export manufactured products. Our export trade is, indeed, desirable, in so far as it results from the development of our internal resources; but all attempts to increase it at the expense of the home demand are unwise. Our main dependence for the distribution of our vast and varied productions is, and must be, the home market. Though the ratio of the home demand to the foreign demand varies in different articles, we, as a general fact, export only *eight per cent* of the aggregate value of our manufacturing, mechanical, and agricultural productions. Probably there is no class of the community which is more benefited by protection than the agriculturist. Without such protection, thousands and thousands of people, who are now among the consumers of agricultural products, would have been driven into the ranks of producers; furnishing their own supplies, and reducing, by increased competition, the profits of both the home and the foreign trade. Hitherto, for reasons that will readily occur, the people of the Western and Southern States have been mainly devoted to agriculture and cotton raising; but they have made a good beginning in manufacturing. As their natural advantages are equal, and in some respects superior, to those of the North-Eastern States, the time cannot be far distant when they will see it to be for their interest to manufacture largely for themselves.

Production and distribution are the agencies by which human wants are supplied; and a nation increases in wealth in the ratio that the sum of its production exceeds that of its consumption. The paramount object to be kept in view in shaping our commercial policy should be to develop in the nation its maximum power of *production*. It cannot be denied, however, that in our great centres of trade the paramount idea is *distribution*. Although production and distribution are reciprocally dependent, the former is of primary importance; for, without it, the latter could not take place. In the great marts, the struggle is for results, without much concern as to the means by which they are produced. Were those who mould and give direction to public opinion in commercial communities to consider more thoroughly the conditions of production on which the prosperity of the country depends, we should have less of that unpractical reasoning which now so largely misleads the popular judgment.

There is nothing more certain in human affairs than that the adoption of free-trade by the United States at their present stage of progress would largely diminish their productive power, reduce the volume of their trade, both foreign and domestic, and consequently lessen their general prosperity. We may suppose that there are not many among us bold enough openly to advocate the prostration of American industry; yet every orator and writer who advocates our adoption of free-trade virtually does that.

EFFORTS OF ENGLAND TO INFLUENCE THE TARIFF POLICY OF OTHER COUNTRIES.

I have already intimated that, in inaugurating the tariff reform in England, her statesmen were influenced more by the exigencies of her situation than by a belief in the virtue of free-trade principles. If they had believed that free-trade is absolutely right, and protection absolutely wrong, without qualification, why did they not at once purge England's tariff of all protective duties? Why did they impose protective duties on many articles of manufacture as late as 1859? Why did they retain protective duties on manufactures of silk till 1860, — fourteen years after they had publicly professed the free-trade faith? Free-trade in corn (breadstuffs) being the chief corner-stone of the free-trade movement, why did they continue to collect a duty on that article which amounted to more than *four millions of dollars* [1] in 1869, — the year of its final repeal? To these interrogatories, one of two answers must be true: these duties were retained either for revenue, or with a wise discrimination as to the fitness of time and circumstances for their repeal. Both of these answers are inconsistent with the canons of free-trade. The free-trader says, that, while it is right to raise revenue by customs duties, it is wrong to impose such duties on articles produced in the country imposing the duty: and yet all the articles to which

[1] When the "corn law" was repealed in 1846, a duty of one shilling per quarter was imposed on corn, which was continued till 1869.

these interrogatories relate are of that class ; that is, they are produced in England. Discrimination as to fitness of time and circumstances in removing or imposing customs duties is the fundamental idea of protection.

Whatever may have been the motives which actuated the free-trade leaders, it is certain that their free-trade professions have been a powerful means of aiding their cause. Thousands of orators and writers who never would — perhaps never could — have discussed the tariff question on practical grounds, being fascinated by the "glittering generalities" which surround the free-trade theory, have become its most zealous advocates. If these astute leaders intended, by their free-trade professions, to enlist in advocacy of British interests this class of orators and writers, it must be admitted that in the United States they have met with some success.

That one great end of the free-trade movement, and especially of the way in which it has been paraded before the world, was and is to influence the commercial regulations of other nations, is shown, not only by the internal evidence and circumstances of the case, but by the declarations of those who were prime movers in the affair. Some of these declarations appear in the following citations. I have Italicized certain phrases worthy of note.

In his speech, opening the great debate of 1846, on the commercial policy of England, Sir Robert Peel, after referring to the protective duties of other countries, said : —

" You have defied the regulations of those countries. . . . But your efforts, whatever be the tariffs of other countries, or however apparent the ingratitude with which they have treated you, — your export trade has been constantly increasing. By the remission of your duties upon raw materials, by increasing your skill and industry, by competition with foreign goods, you have defied your competitors in foreign markets, and you have even been able to exclude them. . . . I say, therefore, to you, that those hostile tariffs, so far from being an objection to continuing your policy, are an argument in its favor. *But, depend upon it, your example will ultimately prevail.*" [1]

---

[1] Hansard, vol. lxxxiii., 3d series, p. 277.

And again, on the fifth night of the adjourned debate, Sir Robert closed his remarkable speech in these words : —

" Choose your motto : ' advance,' or ' recede.' Determine for ' advance,' and it will be the *watchword* that will animate and encourage in every State the friends of liberal commercial policy. Sardinia has taken the lead ; Naples is relaxing ; Prussia is shaken. The French government will be strengthened, and will, perhaps, prevail at last over the self-interest of the commercial and manufacturing aristocracy that now predominates in her chambers. *Can you doubt that the United States will soon relax her hostile tariff,* and that the friends of a freer commercial intercourse — the friends of peace between the two countries — will hail with satisfaction *the example of England.*" [1]

Mr. Gladstone, in his " Remarks on Recent Commercial Legislation," writes : —

" I have dwelt long on this subject of the commercial policy of foreign States; but it is one of immense moment. The power of capital, skill, industry, long-established character and connections, sustaining English commerce, bears up against all that has been done. . . . But, if so, it may be naturally asked, Why all this anxiety ? My answer is, that, while I do not believe that we have been losers, relatively to other countries of which I now speak, but hold, on the contrary, that their blows have told most severely on themselves, yet I cannot doubt that the States in question have taken much from us as well as from their own inhabitants ; have neutralized or contracted a thousand benefits which it was practicable to have attained ; *and that their policy demands from us a vigorous and steady counteraction.* But what is to be the form of that counteraction ? Are we to weary them by remonstrances into undoing their acts ? But first, as matters now stand, *it is too probable that we should be interpreted by contraries, as Irish pigs are said to understand their drivers ;* that the earnestness of our request might be deemed the most demonstrative reason against its being granted. . . . There remains, I think, only one course : it is to use every effort to disburden of all charges, so far as our law is concerned, the materials of industry, and thus to enable the

---

[1] Hansard, vol. lxxxiii., 3d series, p. 1036.

workman to approach his work at home on better terms, as the terms on which he enters foreign markets are altered for the worse against him. . . . *It is this regard to the course of commerce and of commercial legislation in the world at large* which convinces me of the wisdom of pushing further than might otherwise be necessary, or even desirable, our efforts to relieve the materials of industry from fiscal burdens."

We have a later and a very striking exposition of British policy, as designed to act on the commercial regulations of other countries, in a letter from Mr. Gladstone to Mr. Hadfield. In 1856, a conference of the Great Powers was about to sit in Paris for the negotiation and establishment of peace ; and the Manchester Chamber of Commerce requested the Earl of Clarendon (who was to represent Great Britain) to use his influence in that body for the promotion of commercial freedom in Europe by diplomatic means. A similar movement was on foot at Sheffield ; and it was in reference to its expediency that Mr. Gladstone was consulted, and replied, in part, as follows : —

"I strongly sympathize with the feeling which has prompted the Chamber of Commerce at Manchester to present a memorial to Lord Clarendon, with a view to his using his influence, at the approaching congress, in furtherance of commercial freedom in Europe. I am also confident that they will find Lord Clarendon most anxious to give effect to their views. Nor can I desire in any manner to discourage your constituents at Sheffield from following the example which has been set at Manchester. At the same time, I feel bound to point out a danger, the existence of which I too well know from experience.

"Between 1841 and 1845, I held office in the Board of Trade ; and this was the period during which England was most actively engaged in the endeavor to negotiate, with the principal States of the civilized world, treaties for the reciprocal reduction of duties upon imports. *The task was plied on our side with sufficient zeal ; but, in every case, we failed. I am sorry to add my opinion, that we did more than fail.* The whole operation seemed to place us in a false position. Its tendency was to lead countries to regard with jealousy and suspicion, as boons to foreigners, alterations in their laws, which, though doubtless of advantage to foreigners, would have been of far greater advantage to their own inhabitants.

"England, *finding that she could make no progress in this direction, took her own course; struck rapid and decisive blows at the system of protection;* and reduced, as far as the exigencies of the public service would permit, the very high duties, which in many cases she maintained simply for the purpose of revenue, upon articles that had no domestic produce to compete with. While our reasoning had done nothing, or less than nothing, our example effected something at least, if less than we could have desired : and commercial freedom has made some progress in other countries since the year 1846; whereas shortly before that time, even while we were relaxing our tariff, it had actually lost ground.

"When we endeavored to make treaties, we were constantly obstructed by the idea, prevailing abroad, that the reduction of tariffs would redound to our advantage only, and would be detrimental to other countries. Politicians and speculatists continued to propagate this idea. It was certainly shaken, when the world saw us *expose our own protected interests to competition, without making a condition of corresponding relaxation elsewhere;* but I am fearful lest it should again make head, if we too actively employ political influence in urging the adoption of measures for the relaxation of foreign tariffs."

The substance of this remarkable confession of a Prime Minister of England is as follows : "England first endeavored to negotiate, with the principal States of the civilized world, treaties for the reciprocal reduction of duties on imports. The task was plied on her side with sufficient zeal; but in every case she failed." "Finding that she could make no progress in this direction," she then devised the free-trade scheme, and "struck rapid and decisive blows at the system of protection." And, although "her reasoning had done nothing, or less than nothing," she hoped that, "when the world saw her expose her own protected interests to competition, without making a condition of corresponding relaxation elsewhere," her example would prevail. Viewed in connection with the actual condition of Great Britain at the time referred to by Mr. Gladstone, there is something Quixotic in England "striking rapid and decisive blows at the system of protection." The largest protected interest in England was that of corn (breadstuffs) ; and I have already shown that the repeal of the corn laws and the removal of the duties on raw materials were acts of *necessity*, and were in fact only another way of protecting her manufactures. I have also shown that the only duties on her leading manufactures which operated protectively were those on manufactures of silk ; and *these were retained.* What the example of England, in " exposing her own protected interests to competition without making a condition of corresponding relaxation elsewhere,". really amounts to, or how far it should have influence in shaping the course of the American people, it is needless for me to say.[1] Notwithstanding that England, after so many baffled endeavors to adjust by treaty stipulations her commerce with other nations, seemed to have abandoned the very idea in despair, and notwithstanding the fact that all such stipulations are a direct infringement of that free-trade code which she professedly adopted,[2] she surprised the world by concluding, in 1860, a commercial treaty with France.

---

[1] In 1859, three years after the date of Mr. Gladstone's letter, England collected a larger amount of customs duties on the tobacco she imported from the United States than the United States collected on all the articles of British manufacture which they imported from England.

[2] " Generally speaking, all treaties which determine what the duties on importation and exportation shall be, or which stipulate for preferences, are radically objectionable. Nations ought to regulate their tariffs in whatever mode they judge best for the promotion of their own interests, without being shackled by engagements with others. If foreign powers be all treated alike, none of them has just grounds of complaint; and it can rarely be for the interest of any people to show preferences to one over another." — *McCulloch.*

" A commercial treaty debars Parliament from dealing with financial questions as it ought to do, according to its own unbiassed judgment, unfettered by any foregone conclusions between this country and France, but with reference . only to our own domestic interests." — *Earl Grey, in Debate on the Anglo-French Treaty of* 1860. See *Hansard*, vol. clvi. 3d series, p. 1118.

" But what is to be thought of a free-trader who approves, in general, of treaties of commerce ? Did the honorable gentleman ever read the motion made by Mr. Ricardo, when that eminent person, skilled in political economy, said : ' We want trade ; not treaties of commerce, for they are opposed to our principles ?' . . . Why, the very thing itself (a commercial treaty) is a contradiction of your creed." — *Mr. Whiteside : Debate in House of Commons on Anglo-French Treaty.* See *Hansard*, vol. clvi. 3d series, p. 1640.

· That a purpose and hope to influence other countries —
countries, perhaps, whose trade would be more valuable than
that of France is ever likely to be — was one of the motives
which prompted English statesmen in negotiating the Anglo-
French Treaty, is rendered more than probable by the following remarks of Mr. Cobden. They are part of a letter to the
Mayor of Manchester, written soon after Mr. Cobden returned
from Paris : —

" We are not, I trust, taking too sanguine a view of the effects
of the recent commercial arrangement, in assuming that *its influence will be felt beyond the limits of the two countries immediately
concerned.* When England and France are found co-operating,
whether in peace or in war, for the attainment of a common object, *they cannot fail to make their policy triumphant throughout
Europe ;* and, looking at the negotiations now going on elsewhere,
and the indications generally manifested, I am led to the conclusion that, ere long, *the example of those two nations will induce the
whole Continent to adopt a more liberal commercial policy.* In
the mean time, whatever hesitation there may be in Europe, or
whatever *temporary backsliding there may be in America,* it is satis-
factory to know that England, speaking through the voice of Manchester, remains faithful to the principles of unconditional freedom
of trade. If it be accompanied with reciprocity from other countries, so much the better for her and them ; if not, so much the
better for her than them."

English diplomacy — aided, no doubt, by the action of
France, as Mr. Cobden anticipated — has worried other Continental nations into negotiating commercial treaties ; but some
of those nations, after giving the treaty stipulations a fair
trial, express dissatisfaction with their effects.

Speeches in Parliament and the diplomacy of Downing
Street are not the only means the English employ to induce
the nations with which England deals to favor the free admission of her productions. By articles in the reviews and
magazines, by essays and editorials in the daily press, and by
personal discussions with strangers who visit her shores for
pleasure or for business, the folly of those nations which im-

pose protective duties on imports is brought into unseemly prominence. Many will recall with a smile the unsuccessful attempt of the English, at the Centennial Exhibition, to discredit our tariff, by ticketing their goods with prices *with* and *without* customs duties.

Although they often — too often — assert it, are we to believe that these unceasing efforts of the English to influence the commercial regulations of other countries are prompted by motives of philanthropy? The facts which I have adduced forbid such a belief. When we consider what I have before stated, that, to subsist her population, Great Britain must annually import articles for food to the value of over *eight hundred millions of dollars;* that to pay for these articles she must also import raw materials, to be used in manufacture, to the value of nearly *seven hundred millions of dollars,* and annually find a foreign market for her manufactured products to the value of, at least, *twelve hundred millions of dollars,* — we at once see the real ground of her anxiety to extend the area of free-trade. As a successful rivalry in neutral markets would be fatal to her prosperity, her struggle for manufacturing supremacy is, in fact, a struggle for national life. It springs from the strongest motives of human action, — the law of self-preservation. To imagine that, under the circumstances, she will neglect to employ any and every influence likely, in her opinion, to retard the manufacturing progress of other countries, is to expect from her a degree of disinterestedness and philanthropic virtue not to be looked for in any nation. I do not deny her right to use any and all the means she has used to defend her own interests; indeed, it would have been strange had she done otherwise. But that so many of our countrymen should innocently walk into the net so adroitly spread for them, lay aside their patriotism, and advocate free-trade because the English advocate it, use the same arguments for its adoption in the United States that were used for its adoption in England, *irrespective* of the widely different condition of the two countries; and, confounding the advocacy of British interests with philanthropic endeavor, hob-nob with the Cobden Club, and, in obedience

to its behests, seek to organize similar clubs in this country,
— is, to say the least, very remarkable.   It would be simply
ludicrous, were it not a serious matter, to see so many of our
fellow-men in a state of actual delusion in regard to a common-
sense, practical, business question.

With the free-trade *doctrinaire*, I have no controversy.
However plausible his theory may seem, it has no practical
value. It presupposes a condition of things that does not
exist, nor is it probable ever will exist.   It ignores all idea of
patriotism, of national pride, and of national interests.

"If all the countries of the globe were actually, or were
ready to become, constituent portions of one and the same
great family, the theory of free-traders might seem plausible.
But the plain truth is, that the whole analogy is forced and
unnatural.   By treating the human race as one great family,
we are not following, but departing from, the apparent design
of Providence, as indicated in the dispensations that every-
where present themselves to our observation.   In these, we
are totally unable to discover any trace of the ideal corpora-
tion. . . . The Deity seems to have stamped on the features
of Nature and of humanity, in unmistakable characters, that
nations shall remain separate and distinct, each pursuing,
under the restraints only of moral obligations and just laws,
its own interests ; and thus, in beautiful harmony with the
similar arrangements among individuals of the same nation,
each, however unconsciously, contributing to that general
good which is but the aggregate of the separate good of all
the parts." [1]

If, then, it is a part of the Divine economy for the human
race to organize itself into separate communities called nations,
the right to protect and defend national interests must also
be a part of the same Divine arrangement.   There is no more
reason to expect the adoption of universal free-trade than of
universal peace.   Both theories rest on substantially the same
grounds.   When the world (if ever) is in a condition to
practise the one, it will be in a condition to practise the other ;

---

[1] London Quarterly Review, No. 171, p. 86.

but, till then, it is as much the duty of a nation to defend its industries by customs duties, as it is to defend its territory by force of arms.

CONCLUSION.

Let it be deeply and widely impressed on the popular mind, let it be adopted as an axiom by our government, that the nation which produces the most in proportion to its numbers will be the most prosperous and powerful nation. That our natural advantages for the attainment of so important a result are all that could be desired, no one will question. It rests with ourselves to determine whether those advantages shall be turned to the best account. To that end, it is necessary that we should diversify industry, and thereby give employment to all the people, according to their tastes and capacities.

I have dwelt much on the fact, that the great manufacturing industries which enrich nations and promote the welfare of the people cannot expand and prosper here, unless the disparities against us in the great industrial contest are counteracted by customs duties. It is also necessary that we should have an unwavering public policy. For the best results in any pursuit, it is necessary that those who engage in it should possess a well-grounded confidence in the wisdom and stability of legislation ; and in no department, probably, of human affairs is such confidence so necessary or so useful as in the prosecution of manufacturing industry. Such confidence the English manufacturer has always enjoyed. Alike in peace and in war, and under all administrations, he has been able to rely upon the steady and enlightened co-operation of his government. How different in this regard is the position of the American manufacturer ! His government is sometimes hostile (though unwittingly so), sometimes friendly, and sometimes indifferent to the needs of manufacturing industry ; and, at all times, partisan and theoretical discussion so misleads the popular judgment as to make him distrustful in regard to its future action. We cannot attain the high position as a manufacturing nation to which our opportunities entitle us, unless our tariff policy becomes more intelligent in purpose and more uniform in character. Surely the settlement of so momentous a question should no longer be left to chance legislation. The general requirements of production; the relations and reciprocal dependence of the producer and the distributor; the statistics of our own trade, agriculture, manufactures, and other industries, and similar statistics in regard to all the great commercial and producing countries, — are among the facts which our legislators need to know, and without which they cannot safely act.

The question must be removed from the narrow arena of partisan politics, of sectional and individual selfishness. There is one safe ground which we may all take, — one broad ground on which we can all stand, — and that is, the American ground. Let us ever remember that it is our own country, and not some other country, whose interests are intrusted to our keeping. Providence has not imposed upon us the impossible task of looking after the rest of the world. In taking proper care of ourselves, — always, however, with strict regard to the unchanging rules of honor and justice and to the best dictates of humanity, — we shall, as a nation, pursue the path that leads, not only to wealth and happiness at home, but to respect and influence abroad. It is the nation of great internal resources, of vigorous productive power and self-dependent strength, which is always best prepared and most able, not only to defend itself, but to lend others a helping hand. It is by conforming to the plain teachings of common sense and experience, not by listening to the dreamy suggestions of a chimerical cosmopolitanism, that we are to raise our country to its proper place among the nations, — a place which, if we are true to ourselves, will be second to no other in arts or in arms.

APPENDIX.

APPENDIX.

In establishing an American tariff policy, the following citations of the views held by some of the ablest statesmen of our day, and the wisest of those who laid the foundations of the Republic, are worthy of thoughtful consideration. Dr. FRANKLIN, writing from London in 1771, to HUMPHREY MARSHALL, used the following language : —

"Every manufacturer encouraged in our country makes part of a *market* for provisions within ourselves, and saves so much money to the country as must otherwise be exported to pay for the manufactures he supplies. Here, in England, it is well known and understood that, wherever a manufacture is established which employs a number of hands, it raises the value of land in the neighboring country all around it; partly by the greater demand near at hand for the produce of the land, and partly from the plenty of money drawn by the manufacturers to that part of the country. It seems, therefore, the interest of all our farmers and owners of lands to encourage our young manufactures in preference to foreign ones imported among us from distant countries."

In 1815, THOMAS JEFFERSON wrote as follows to J. B. SAY : —

"Experience has shown, that continued peace depends not merely on our own justice and prudence, but on that of others also ; that, when forced into a war, the interception of exchanges which must be made across a wide ocean becomes a powerful weapon in the hands of an enemy domineering over that element, and, to other distresses of war, adds the want of all those necessaries for which we have permitted ourselves to be dependent on others, — even arms and clothing. This fact, therefore, solves the question, by reducing to its ultimate form, whether profit or preservation is the first interest of the State ? We are consequently become manufacturers to a degree incredible to those who do not see it, and who only consider the short period of time during which we have been driven to them by the suicidal policy of England. The prohibitory duties we lay on all articles of foreign manufacture which prudence requires us to establish at home, with the patriotic determination of every good citizen to use no foreign article which can be made within ourselves, without regard to difference of prices, secures us against relapse into foreign dependency."

The constitutionality of our protective laws was strongly affirmed and conclusively argued by JAMES MADISON; and no one certainly could speak on such points with more authority. In a letter to JOSEPH C. CABELL, dated Sept. 18, 1828, Mr. MADISON thus winds up the long and convincing argument : —

" A further evidence in support of the constitutional power to protect and foster manufactures by regulations of trade — an evidence that ought of itself to settle the question — is the uniform and practical sanction given to the power by the general government for nearly forty years, with a concurrence or acquiescence of every State government throughout the same period ; and, it may be added, through all the vicissitudes of party which marked that period. No novel construction, however ingeniously devised, or however respectable and patriotic its patrons, can withstand the weight of such authorities, or the unbroken current of so prolonged and universal a practice; and well is it that this cannot be done without the intervention of the same authority which made the Constitution. ' If it could be so done, there would be an end to that stability in government and in laws which is essential to good government and good laws, — a stability the want of which is the imputation which has, at all times, been levelled against republicanism with most effect."

In a letter to the same individual, written a few weeks later, Mr. MADISON thus alludes to the *laissez faire* doctrine, and to the fallacy of free-trade : —

" The theory of ' let us alone ' supposes that all nations concur in a perfect freedom of commercial intercourse. Were this the case, they would, in a commercial view, be but one nation, as much as the several districts composing a particular nation; and the theory would be as applicable to the former as to the latter. But this golden age of free-trade has not yet arrived, nor is there a single nation that has set the example. No nation can, indeed, safely do so, until a reciprocity at least be insured to it. . . . A nation leaving its foreign trade, in all cases, to regulate itself, might soon find it regulated by other nations into subserviency to a foreign interest. In the interval between the peace of 1783 and the establishment of the present Constitution of the United States, the want of a general authority to regulate trade is known to have had this consequence. . . . The theory supposes, moreover, a perpetual peace; a supposition, it is to be feared, not less chimerical than a universal freedom of commerce."

Few of our great men have left behind them a deeper impression of their practical sagacity than ANDREW JACKSON. Read what, in 1824, he wrote to Dr. COLMAN: —

"You ask my opinion on the tariff. I answer, that I am in favor of a judicious examination and revision of it; and so far as the tariff-bill before us embraces the design of fostering, protecting, and preserving within ourselves the means of national defence and independence, particularly in a state of war, I would advocate and support it. The experience of the late war ought to teach us a lesson, and one never to be forgotten. If our liberty and republican form of government procured for us by our Revolutionary fathers are worth the blood and treasure at which they were obtained, it surely is our duty to protect and defend them. . . . This tariff — I mean a judicious one — possesses more fanciful than real danger. I will ask, What is the real situation of the agriculturist? Where has the American farmer a market for his surplus product? Except for cotton, he has neither a foreign nor home market. Does not this clearly prove, when there is no market either at home or abroad, that there is too much labor employed in agriculture, and that the channels for labor should be multiplied? Common sense points out the remedy. Draw from agriculture the superabundant labor; employ it in mechanism and manufactures, thereby creating a home market for your breadstuffs, and distributing labor to the most profitable account and benefits to the country. Take from agriculture, in the United

States, six hundred thousand men, women, and children, and you will at once give a home market for more breadstuffs than all Europe now furnishes us. In short, sir, we have been too long subject to the policy of British merchants. It is time that we should become a little more *Americanized*, and, instead of feeding the paupers and laborers of England, feed our own; or else, in a short time, by continuing our present policy, we shall be rendered paupers ourselves."

In his second annual message to Congress (Dec. 7, 1830), President JACKSON closes an argument in favor of the constitutional right to so adjust the customs duties as to encourage domestic industry, with these words : —

"In this conclusion, I am confirmed as well by the opinions of Presidents WASHINGTON, JEFFERSON, MADISON, and MONROE, who have each repeatedly recommended the exercise of this right under the Constitution, as by the uniform practice of Congress, the continual acquiescence of the States, and the general understanding of the people."

DANIEL WEBSTER, addressing, in 1833, the mechanics and manufacturers of Buffalo, spoke as follows : —

"Desiring always to avoid extremes, and to observe a prudent moderation in regard to the protective system, I yet hold steadiness and perseverance in maintaining what has been established to be essential to the public prosperity. Nothing can be worse than that what concerns the daily labor and the daily bread of whole classes of the people should be subject to frequent and violent changes. It were far better not to move at all, than to move forward, and then fall back again.

"My sentiments, gentlemen, on the tariff question are generally known. In my opinion, a just and a leading object in the whole system is the encouragement and protection of American manual labor. I confess that every day's experience convinces me more and more of the high propriety of regarding this object. Our government is made for all, not for a few. Its object is to promote the greatest good of the whole; and this ought to be kept constantly in view in its administration. The far greater number of those who maintain the government belong to what may be called the industrious or productive classes of the community. With us, labor is not depressed, ignorant, and unintelligent: on the contrary, it is active, spirited, enterprising, seeking its own rewards, and laying up for its own competence and its own support. The motive to labor is the great stimulus to our whole society, and no system is wise or just which does not afford this stimulus as far as it may. The protection of American labor against the injurious competition of foreign labor, so far at least as respects general handicraft productions, is known historically to have been one end designed to be obtained by establishing the Constitution; and this object, and the constitutional power to accomplish it, ought never to be surrendered or compromised in any degree."

In his farewell Address, WASHINGTON thus points out the danger of conforming National policy to cosmopolitan ideas: —

" It is folly in one nation to look for disinterested favors from another; that it must pay, with a portion of its independence, for whatever it may accept under that character; that, by such acceptance, it may place itself in the condition of having given equivalents for nominal favors, and yet of being reproached with ingratitude for not giving more. There can be no greater error than to expect, or calculate upon, real favors from nation to nation. It is an illusion which experience must cure, which a just pride ought to discard."

Cambridge: Press of John Wilson & Son.